HORRIBLE HISTORIES

OXFORD

TERRY DEARY

Illustrated by Martin Brown

For Roger and Julia King. TD

To Victoria Garrard, a delightful colleague...

...and paste-up slave. MB

Scholastic Children's Books
Euston House
24 Eversholt Street
London
NW1 1DB

A division of Scholastic Ltd
London ~ New York ~ Toronto ~ Sydney ~ Auckland
Mexico City ~ New Delhi ~ Hong Kong

Published in the UK by Scholastic UK Ltd, 2007

10 digit ISBN: 0 439 95394 4
13 digit ISBN: 978 0439 95394 8

Printed and bound by GGP Media GmbH Pößneck, Germany

2 4 6 8 10 9 7 5 3 1

CONTENTS

INTRODUCTION

Lots of cities have nicknames.

London is 'The Smoke' ... because it used to be smoky...

Chicago is 'The Windy City' because it is windy...

But poor old Oxford, in the heart of England, is known as...

A poet called Malcolm Arnold (1822–88) gave it that name. Now that is just plain stupid, Mr Arnold. Let's be honest.

Spires are the pointy hats you put on buildings. They do NOT dream. And, if they did, what would they dream about?

But the history of Oxford is so horrible the spires would not be having sweet dreams – they'd be having nightmares.

It was in the Oxford estate of Blackbird Leys that riots were going on in the 1990s when car thieves were racing police through the streets ... and winning!

But the horrors of Oxford are much older than that. So welcome to the REAL history of Oxford ... the *horrible* history...

Oxford's twisted timeline

AD **600s** First Christians settle at Oxford and build a monastery. St Frideswide (650–735) hides from the man who wants to marry her in an Oxford pigsty. Miracles happen. St Frid dies.

AD **911** Oxford people are scared of raids from the Danes so they build the first wall around the town.

1002 Peaceful Viking settlers in Oxford are massacred by the local English, so-o-o…

1009 …vicious Vikings burn down Oxford in revenge. Viking King Sweyn takes over for a while.

1071 The Norman knight Robert d'Oilly is given land at Oxford and builds the first Oxford Castle. But a Norman book says the town is 'waste'. An Oilly waste. Yeuch. But d'Oilly builds a bridge so Oxford becomes a popular place to cross the river Thames without getting wet.

1132 King Henry I builds a palace in Oxford (where Beaumont Street is now). He spends the summer there.

1135 Henry's dead and his nephew (Stephen) and his daughter (Matilda) scrap for the throne. Oxford is a battleground.

1142 Queen Matilda is trapped in Oxford Castle and surrounded by the army of her enemy, Stephen. Just before the food runs out she is lowered from the castle on a rope and escapes over the snow-covered fields. She is not spotted because she wears a white cloak for camouflage.

Matilda escaping

1263 Local nobleman John de Balliol starts building a college. Balliol had insulted the Bishop of Durham – this is his way of saying, 'Sorry, Bish'.

THAT'S VERY NICE BUT A BUNCH OF FLOWERS WOULD HAVE DONE

1258 Simon de Montfort and 23 other rebel barons hold a meeting in Oxford. The rebels force King Henry III to change the way England is ruled. There will be a parliament in London. Henry has to agree to 'The Provisions of Oxford'[1]. They say the king has to listen to a 'council' of wise Englishmen. Sounds boring.

BLAH BLAH BLAH BLAH BLAH BLAH BLAH BLAH BLAH BLAH BLAH BLAH BLAH BLAH BLAH BLAH BLAH

I LIKED OXFORD BETTER WHEN IT WAS A WASTE

1355 The St Scholastica Day riots start on 10 February. Not the first but the worst of the riots where Oxford people fought against students.

1555 Queen Mary Tudor has two bishops and an archbishop burned outside Oxford city walls. Frying tonight.

LOUSY TOWNY

PUTRID PUPIL

1 Sadly Henry later changed his mind. The barons went to war ... and lost. Simon lost his head as well as the war ... and that is painful.

8

1646 King Charles is fighting the Civil War and makes Oxford his capital. Roundhead enemies attack. Charles makes his escape on the night of 27 April. On 24 June the Roundheads march in. Oxford surrenders. End of Civil War.

1683 The Ashmolean Museum, designed by Christopher Wren, opens. It's the world's first university museum and on display is the body of the last dodo bird seen in Europe. By 1755 all that is left of the bird is the head and a foot!

1840s The Great Western Railway links Oxford with London. Lots of filthy coal smoke to choke the Oxford people and blacken the buildings. Dreaming spires become the need-cleaning spires.

1954 Roger Bannister, a medical student, becomes the first person to run a mile in under four minutes. A new record. Maybe he'd robbed a bank?

2002 Radio listeners vote Cornmarket Street the second worst street in Britain. The following year the street is repaved and new benches are added.

SAINTS AND SKELETONS

St Frideswide is the saint of Oxford, and she lived from about AD 650 to 735 .

People came from miles around to see her grave – people are a bit odd like that. These visitors helped Oxford to grow long before the students and colleges were built.

Frideswide's fan club
You may think a saint has to be a sweet and kind person. But Frid was pretty foul to one of her fans.

Frideswide was a nun. King Algar was a tyrant king who fell in love with her saintly mush. He sent messengers to her home in Didcot to ask her to marry him.

How romantic? No. Because nuns don't marry.

Algar didn't give up easily. He became a real pest. Frid ran away to Oxford. Algar followed. But when he reached Oxford he suddenly became blind.

Algar said, 'Sorry, Frid!' and she gave him his sight back. (Saints can do miracles like that.)

He gave up and left her alone. She went off to a pigsty to pray. This is NOT where the horrible historical joke comes from...

A monastery sprang up around the holy lady. Lots of miracles happened at St Frideswide's monastery – Frid cured a man of leprosy.

When Frideswide died she was buried in the monastery in a fine 'shrine' ... that's a posh, stone tomb. The tomb of the saint was a popular place for Christians to visit.

There were new taverns and shops to give food and shelter to the visitors.

Oxford had its first 'tourists' ... and it still has them.

In the 1530s Henry VIII closed the monastery but the monastery church became Oxford Cathedral. In 1538 Frideswide's bones were dumped (because she was a Catholic saint and Henry's Protestants hated Catholic saints).

Her bones were found in 1562 in a corner of the cathedral. They knew it was Frideswide because her bones were wrapped in silk.

On 11 January 1562 Frideswide was buried again at the east end of the cathedral ... along with the Protestant nun, Katherine Martyr. A Protestant nun buried with a Catholic nun! Just *imagine* the rows that must go on in *that* grave!

Well ... well

When Frideswide was hiding from Algar she prayed for water and a spring sprang up. This became a well at Frilsham, and a curious story is told about it.

If you went to the well in the 1800s it was said you would meet a spitting toad.

Girls would take their boyfriends. If the boyfriend was their true love, then he would be safe from the spit.

But an untrue boy would be spat at by the toad.

Did you know…?
Frideswide also had a well at St Margaret's Church, Binsey, which was supposed to cure sick people. The Saxon word for 'cure all' was 'treacle'. So the well was known as the 'Treacle Well' … the cure-all well.

In *Alice's Adventures in Wonderland* Lewis Carroll (1832–98) wrote about a dormouse that lived down a well full of treacle … a treacle well. People thought a treacle well was part of the book's nonsense. It wasn't! There really IS a Treacle Well. Carroll and his little friend Alice often visited St Frideswide's well.

"Who is your new friend?" Alice said to the dormouse…

"Do you want me to spit on her?" said the toad.

VICIOUS FOR VIKINGS

By AD 1002 England was full of Viking settlers. Happy families. Oxford had hundreds of people from Denmark. But then English King Ethelred the Unready said...

The Danes are springing up in England like weeds among the wheat. They must be destroyed. From today the English people can kill anyone from Denmark. It is not against the law.

SOUNDS LIKE PAINS FOR THE DANES

The Danes in Oxford were craftsmen and traders – not Viking warriors. When they heard about the new law they panicked. They rushed to St Frideswide's Church for safety. They broke through the locks and shut themselves in. 'The English won't harm us in a church,' they thought (though they thought it in Danish, of course). B-I-G mistake.

Horrible Histories note: Remember – if someone is out to kill all of your group then SCATTER. Most of you will get away. Do NOT gather in one place. That will make it easy-peasy for your enemies to kill you.

On 13 November 1002 the awful Oxford English simply set fire to the wooden church with the Danes inside it.

The king of Denmark's sister was one of the women who

died, along with her children. The king, Sweyn Forkbeard, was not happy. He probably said that … in Danish.

I AM NOT HAPPY ... IN DANISH

Before long, King Sweyn Forkbeard came with an avenging force of Vikings. They burned the rest of Oxford to the ground.

King Ethelred ran away to France. He only came home when Sweyn Forkbeard died in 1013. Eth had St Frideswide's Church built again. This is the place where Christ Church stands today.

Curious colleges

Oxford is famous for its university. It's the oldest university in Britain. But when did it start?

King Edward III (1327–77) said…

IN ANCIENT TIMES THE GREEKS DEFEATED THE TROJANS. THE TROJANS SAILED OVER TO ENGLAND AND CONQUERED IT. THEN THEY SET UP OXFORD UNIVERSITY

IS ED GETTING SOFT IN THE 'EAD?

Ed was WRONG.

Other people said the famous King Alfred (AD 849 – 899) set up the first college. He didn't.

It probably all started in the mid-1100s with schools at St Frideswide's Monastery – a hundred years before Alf was born. The best teachers moved in and the best students followed.

There WAS a university there in AD 1180 but we'll never know exactly when it started. We do know that it wasn't always fun being a student. Here are some terrible tales of when it was lousy for learners…

1 Horrible houses

In the 1300s students were living in cheap and overcrowded inns and lodging houses.

Nice.

2 Dead duck

All Souls College was built in 1438. There is a story that says the builders dug a hole and a giant mallard duck flew out. Every year the college has a feast, and at the first feast of every century the students grab sticks and torches and hunt for the ghost of the mallard. They look all around the college and even on the rooftops. They end by singing the 'Mallard Song'.

'Swapping' means 'wonderful'.

The last mallard hunt was in 2001 and the next will be held in 2101 – so you'll have a long wait to see it.

3 Teacher cheaters

The students of University College always said their college was the very first to be built. They said…

> KING ALFRED THE GREAT BUILT THIS COLLEGE IN AD 872

In 1872 they had a 1000th birthday party.

But it was all a lie! The college was built in the 1200s. The teachers had papers that said 'This land was given by King Alfred in AD 872'. But it DOESN'T say there was a college there.

4 Poo phew!

New College was built in 1379 with a large toilet block, the Long Room. It didn't have sewers under its toilets. All the toilet waste fell into a huge pit.

The pit was so big it was the biggest in the history of Oxford.

> POO
> ~~NEW~~ COLLEGE

The pit was so huge it held the poo from New for 300 years before it filled up. Then someone had the lovely job of emptying it.

Who? We don't know … but I bet the people of Oxford could smell who dunnit.

5 Smelly for students

A corpse soon starts to rot. It gets very smelly.

So if you had a dead teacher lying around your school you would know after a couple of days, wouldn't you?

But on 19 February 1386 the body of Edmund Strete, a University College teacher was found hidden in the straw of his bedding.

The law officers decided Strete had been murdered FIVE WEEKS before, on 10 January. His servant John West was probably the killer. He'd run away.

But why didn't the other people in the college smell the corpse? Because the college was already such a smelly place?

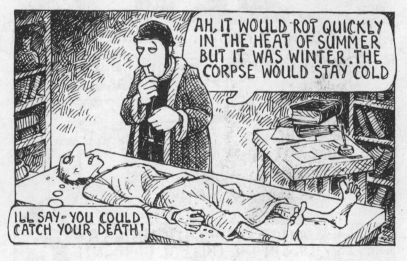

6 Terrible tutors

The Oxford students have had some weird teachers through history.

William Archibald Spooner (1844–1930) taught at Oxford for 60 years. He was famous for mixing up the sounds at the beginning of words.

So what? So he came up with some comical mistakes. Some of his most famous mix-ups were…

People enjoyed making up 'Spoonerisms'. So they'd come up with clever stories like this…

ONE DAY I TOOK OUT MY WELL-BOILED ICICLE AND WENT FOR A RIDE. THEN IT STARTED ROARING WITH PAIN. MY TIRELESS TUBE BUST AND A CAT POPPED ON ITS DRAWERS IN FRONT OF ME! I SWERVED BUT STRUCK THE CAT A BLUSHING CROW. THE CAT RAN OFF WITH A WITTY-FULL PAIL AND HISS

Me what I seen?

But was Spooner REALLY as bad as people said?

The truth is that people were writing Spoonerisms before the Reverend Spooner was even born. A 1622 book describes how a man in an inn said…

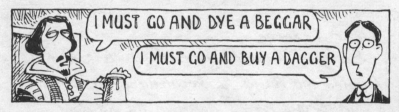

I MUST GO AND DYE A BEGGAR

I MUST GO AND BUY A DAGGER

A character in an 1854 novel (a year when Spooner was just a boy) invited his friend to 'poke a smipe'.

Poor Spooner never enjoyed being laughed at. As he grew older he grew angrier. A large crowd showed up for one lecture and he raged…

YOU HAVEN'T COME FOR MY LECTURE, YOU JUST WANT TO HEAR ONE OF THOSE…THINGS

Sad.

HE THIGHED IN NINETEEN-DIRTY

BURNING BISHOPS

In the 1530s Henry VIII closed down the Catholic monasteries and made all the churches follow his new religion - Protestantism.

His daughter, Mary Tudor, was still a Catholic. So, when Henry died and Mary came to the throne she turned England Catholic again. Anyone who stayed a Protestant was punished. The top Protestants were burned. There were three famous burnings in Oxford.

What sort of person could burn another human? Could you? If the executioner could write, then a letter home may have looked a bit like this…

Dear George
Sorry I haven't written for a while but I burned me hand. Executing Protestants is a dangerous job. I mean, in the old days I shoved the criminals up a ladder, popped a rope round their necks and turned the ladder so they dropped. Cccckt! Easy and painless. Well, not painless for the criminal - some of them took ten minutes to die - but painless for me.

Now good Queen Mary (God bless her) wants these Protestant priests burned alive.

She wants to put on a bit of a show. We had two last month — two bishops. Top men. Big crowds. And me the star of the show.

The two were Bishop Latimer and Bishop Ridley.

First I gets the lads to build a scaffold and I plants a nice couple of poles in it. Then I builds a pile of wood round them. I puts on me mask so nobody knows who I am — and off I go to get the prisoners from the prison in the North Gate.

Now, George, this is where the clever bit comes. I hangs a bag of gunpowder round the prisoners' neck. See? Flames reach bag. Boom! Bye-bye Bishop! The crowd likes that bit.

Anyway, I ties their hands and I leads them down the streets to Broad Street, outside the city walls — It has to be outside the city. The ladies hang their washing on lines in the city. They don't want soot from burnt bishops on their petticoats, do they?

"As I was saying, I takes the bishops out – the crowds aren't cheering or jeering or nothing. Ridley talks to his friends and gives them little coins and nutmegs. Nice old feller.

Very quiet execution it is. I ties them to the poles – the bishops, not the crowds, that is – and after all the usual prayers and things I strikes a light and lights me torch.

Fine words. They brings a tear to me eye – or it could have been the smoke from the torch blowing in me face.

That's when I lights old Latimer's fire and I did a good job. Old Latimer was 70 years old. Burning him was no trouble. He was dry as an old stick anyway! Crackle, sizzle bang and the old bloke is gone. But Ridley is different. Don't blame me! The crowd tried to say it was my fault, you know. I ran out of dry sticks, didn't I? Well, it was 16 October and a damp time of year. Ridley's sticks were a bit on the wet side. They smokes a lot. They burns slowly... and so does he. Oh, dear

The screams would give you nightmares.

At last the ropes burn through and he falls forward into the fire. That sets off the gunpowder and finishes him off. Splatters him a bit.

Of course I had to push the bits back in the fire. That's when I burns me hand.

Some people were muttering about the Queen, calling her Bloody Mary (God bless her) and some were calling me even worse names for using damp wood! It was the weather. Don't blame me! I was only doing me job. I just wish her blessed Majesty would go back to hanging them. Much neater. Much safer - well not for the victims - they ends up dead either way! Safer for me though.

Time to change me bandage. Hope to see you at Christmas.

Love to Bess and the kids.

Your loving brother

Harry

Hopeless hand

Archbishop Thomas Cranmer knew he was next. He had watched his friends Latimer and Ridley die horribly.

He was locked in the North Gate and lost his nerve. 'I'll become a Catholic!' he whinged.

'Sign this paper to show you mean it,' the Catholics told him.

Cranmer signed. 'Thanks. Now we're going to burn you anyway! Hah!'

Five months later he went to the stake. Cranmer was cross. When he was burned he stretched out his right hand – the hand that had signed the paper. He wanted to punish the hand for being so wicked[2].

My hand shall first be punished!

Miserable Mary and martyrs' memories

The Protestants made Latimer, Ridley and Cranmer into heroes – people who died for their religion – usually called martyrs. Latimer was remembered as going to his death saying, 'Be of good comfort, Mr Ridley, and play the man. We shall light such a candle it shall never be put out.'

What a shame he probably didn't say that! The story of the burnt bishops was told eight years after their deaths, in 1563. There were no last words. The book was a best-seller. When it was printed again the famous 'such a candle' words were added. They may have been spoken by a Christian martyr 1,400 years before!

2 Of course this is seriously stupid. It was his brain that told his hand to sign. Why didn't he fry his brain? Poor helpless hand.

In the 1800s a Martyrs' Cross was put up in St Giles to remember Latimer, Ridley and Cranmer. In the church, the holes made in the pillars to hold the scaffold are marked with a sign.

But they were actually burned at Broad Street. In the 1800s some Oxford workmen discovered the stump of a stake and pieces of charred bone in Broad Street. A cross on the road marks the spot.

Mary went on to burn 400 more Protestants around England. Then she died ... and England became a Protestant country again, under Elizabeth, her half-sister. Catholics were then martyred for THEIR faith.

THE SAVAGE CIVIL WAR

King Charles I was a bit of a big-head. He told Parliament…

I'M THE KING. I CAN RULE THE COUNTRY WITHOUT THE HELP OF PARLIAMENT. SO SHOVE OFF

The people said…

WE'LL SEE ABOUT THAT

In the end the king's men (the Cavaliers) went to war with Parliament's army (the Roundheads). It's called 'The English Civil War'.

Parliament ruled in London so Charles needed a new capital for the Cavaliers – he settled on Oxford.

Of course old Oxford was battered by the Roundheads.

Here are some 'orrible Oxford tales from those days…

1 The people of Oxford liked the Roundheads, but the colleges of Oxford liked the king and his Cavaliers. The people and the colleges were arguing … as usual.

ROUNDHEAD!

BLOCKHEAD!

2 No one college was big enough for the king and the queen and all their servants. So Charles stayed at Christ Church College and Queen Henrietta stayed at Merton College.

If Charles wanted to see Henrietta he had a l-o-n-g walk. That would never do. So Charles said...

That door is still there today.

3 Oxford was a dangerous place to live during the Civil War. The Cavalier soldiers in the city got bored and drunk every night. They started fighting each other. The king said, 'No booze after nine p.m.'

4 Charles's Cavaliers began to lose the war. The Roundheads began to close in.

FIRST I HAD A LETTER SIGNED BY ROUNDHEAD GENERAL FAIRFAX

HE PINCHED IT FROM A SOLDIER

BORROWED

I CUT MY HAIR, TRIMMED MY BEARD AND DRESSED AS A SERVANT

HE PINCHED MY SPARE CLOTHES

YOU COULD HAVE WASHED THEM

AT MIDNIGHT WE SENT *TWO* SETS OF RIDERS OUT OF OXFORD

ONE WAS A DECOY. SNEAKY

CRAFTY

A MAN SHOUTED AFTER ME... GOODBYE *HARRY!*

I THOUGHT OF THAT NEAT TOUCH

AND I RODE TO THE SAFETY OF SCOTLAND

AND LEFT THE PEOPLE OF OXFORD TO FACE THE DANGER

5 No one knew where Charles had gone. The Roundheads were furious when they found out. They sent out a menacing notice…

Any person who knows where the king is hiding and will not tell is a traitor. They shall die without mercy.

TORTURE ME ALL YOU LIKE I WILL NEVER TELL YOU…

I WILL NEVER TELL YOU… THAT HE IS HEADING FOR SCOTLAND

6 The Scots asked the English for £2 million. They were given £400,000 by the Roundheads[3].

Charles was sent back to England, under arrest. He was kept in Newcastle. This time his escape plan failed. He was then sent to Carisbrooke Castle on the south coast. Another escape plan failed.

3 The Scots SAID they didn't 'sell' Charles I back to England. They SAID they planned to hand Charles over even if they didn't get a penny. Would they? Make up your own mind.

Queen Matilda could have told him. The queen who slipped out of Oxford on a snowy night, dressed in a snow-white cloak[4].

Charles had his head lopped off in London.

Did you know...?
When the Roundheads took over Oxford, they marched into Mrs Fell's college house and told her they were taking over. 'Get out!' they said. 'No,' she told them. 'I am not leaving this armchair.' So they simply picked up the armchair and dumped her outside on the grass. Mrs Fell lost her little battle.

Roundheads rule
In 1650 the Roundheads had won. Roundhead leader, Oliver Cromwell, sacked a lot of the heads of the colleges. Then Cromwell ordered that the city walls and castle be knocked about a bit. His soldiers smashed them. That way Oxford could not be defended again.

4 No, NOT the little girl Snow White – Matilda didn't pinch Snow White's cloak ... and she wasn't helped by seven dwarfs either.

And the tumbling walls were a reminder to the people of Oxford – never cross a Cromwell.

You'll never walk alone

Colonel Francis Windebank was a Royalist and a loser. When the Roundheads marched into Merton College the colonel surrendered … but the Roundheads shot him anyway.

You can still see him today … well, his ghost. Some say he walks around the library on his knees. Others say he is walking on the OLD floor that was lower than the new one. It just LOOKS as if he is on his knees.

Here's how to spot the difference.

1. Colonel Windebank on his knees

2. Colonel Windebank on his feet...but walking on an old floor

3. Colonel Windebank with a hole in his head and not walking anywhere fast

Windebank is not wandering alone.

Archbishop William Laud was beheaded in 1645 for taking sides with King Charles. His headless ghost has been seen in the library of St John's College. The question is, WHERE IS HIS HEAD???

The answer is too horrible to tell you.

Oh, very well. It is rolling along the floor. As he walks along with a candle in his hand he keeps kicking it. Imagine that? Doomed to kick yourself in the head every night. What does the head think about that?

I HAVE NO BODY TO HELP ME

After lots of blood on British fields, and misery for everyone from musketeers to mothers, Charlie got the chop. His head was cut off.

Did you know…?

England was bombed during World War II (1939–45) but Oxford escaped the bombs. Why? Was it just lucky? Maybe not. It is said that the German leader, Adolf Hitler, refused to let his bombers attack Oxford.

Oxford had been the capital of England when Charles I had gone there in the English Civil War. Now Adolf Hitler wanted to make Oxford HIS capital…

VEN I VIN ZE VAR!

Of course he didn't vin ze var … I mean win the war … so ve vill really never know why Oxford kept its dreaming spires.

CUTTING UP CORPSES

In the 1700s you could go to Christ Church College and learn how to be a surgeon.

How did you practise cutting up sick patients? You practised on a corpse.

Where did the corpse come from? From men and women who had been hanged in Oxford.

Oxford people used to go along to the jail to see hangings. They went to see a show. So criminals were hanged in front of the people then cut up in front of the students. Nice.

Horrible hangings

Giles Covington was executed for robbing and murdering a pedlar, David Charteris, on the road home from Abingdon Fair in 1787.

He was caught and hanged four years after the murder, and he went to his death with a rant and a rage. He stood on the ladder with a rope around his neck and said he didn't batter David Charteris to death.

Two other men were accused of killing Charteris and they were hanged together. One of them, Charles Shury, really gave the crowds a show. Shury stood alongside John Castle and began to speak.

Shury went into a fury…

> *Your life will be blown out like a candle and so will all your family!*[5]

Then Castle began to speak…

> **INNOCENT…BLAH …GOD FORGIVE… BLAH!…NEVER KILLED…BLAH!**

In the end, Shury turned the fury on Castle and cried out…

> *For God's sake, hang that fellow or he'll keep talking all the day!*

Both men were hanged and their bodies were left hanging till the next day. Then they were carted off to Christ's College to be carved.

That's what the Oxford crowds went to see. Death and drama.

In 2006 you can STILL see the skeleton of Giles Covington at the Museum of Oxford … if you like looking at skeletons.

> **ARE YOU KIDDING?**

5 We don't know if Shury's curse came true. Probably not.

But there was one criminal who worked out a way to stop the surgeons cutting him up…

Darkin's dirty deeds
Nettlebed is a place just outside Oxford. Would YOU like to live in a place called Nettlebed?

YOU'D NOT WANT TO LIVE IN NETTLEBED IN THE 1700s, NAYYY! IT WERE A DANGEROUS PLACE IN THEM DAYS ARRHH! IF THE NETTLES DIDN'T GET YOU THE HIGHWAYMEN MIGHT

But it was dangerous for the highwaymen too … if they got caught.

THEY COMES OUT OF THE WOODS, ROBS YER AND VANISHES BACK INTO THE TREES. ARRRH! BUT JAMES DURKIN, HE GOT CAUGHT, THE LIRIPOOP [6]

How was Deadly Durkin caught? He wrote a letter to another highwayman. The law officers read the letter and arrested him. What did dipstick Durkin write? Maybe…

6 An Oxford student would wear a liripoop – a sort of tail on the back of his hood. But the word ALSO meant an idiot. Now you know that you are not a liripoop any longer.

Dear Fred

Come and join me in Nettlebed. Robbing has never been so easy. There's enough for the two of us. Take the road from Oxford and turn right at Nettlebed crossroads. My hideout is the third ash tree on the left.

Your old mate,
Jim

P.S. Bring some bottles of beer. I'm sick of this nettle wine.

OF COURSE HE WAS TAKEN TO OXFORD TO BE HANGED AND CUT UP BY THE SURGEONS. ARRHH, BUT HE DIDN'T LIKE THAT AT ALL, NAYYY!

Durkin had an idea…

Dear Fred

Do me one last favour. When I'm hanged get some barge-men to mash my body about so the surgeons can't cut me up. Barge-men are best. They're the strongest men in Britain.

Your late mate,
Jim

P.S. Hope you don't end up like me. No noose is good news, they say.

Durkin had his wish. As his body was hanging some tough men burst through.

38

The barge-men cut down the body and jumped up and down on it till it was mushed.

Why did they do it? Because they were paid.

How much would they have to pay YOU to do that? Two weeks' pocket money at least?

Did you know....?
The last highwayman caught in Nettlebed was 'Curly Bill' Fisher.

He wasn't hanged and jumped on. He was transported to Australia in 1835.

7 It ISN'T. That's just a joke. Barge men worked on the rivers, loading the barges. If you didn't get the joke maybe you're a liripoop after all.

Body guards

In March 1754, Oxford had seen riots when a mob carried off two hanged bodies to stop the surgeons slicing them up. The hangings had been at a place called Green Ditch. (It's St Margaret's Road today.)

In April, Oxford Council put some strong men in front of the scaffold to guard the hanged corpse of James Till. The council orders said…

> *The guards must lay hold of, and lock in the castle, any person who tries to carry off the body*

For Till's execution it worked. James Till was just 27 years old.

The walls of Oxford Castle were falling down by the 1780s. In 1787, they were built up again in a special way. They were too high for most people to climb. But if you stood in the road outside you could see into the castle yard. That meant you could watch a hanging but not get TOO near the corpse.

The last execution at Oxford in public was in 1863.

Did you know…?

The castle was crumbling badly by 1778. A gypsy called Elisabeth Boswell was locked in the castle cells for theft. She managed to…

• Break out of her cell
• Open the locks on the cell of two highwaymen who joined her
• Force her way through the side of St George's Tower
• Lower herself down the outer walls using bed sheets
• Climb over the iron spikes of a ditch into a garden
• Run off

It was her second escape. Each time she was caught within a month. She made her jailer look pretty stupid. And what was her daft jailer called?
a) Locker b) Wisdom c) Nutter

Answer: b) Solomon Wisdom. It seems he didn't have a lot.

QUAINT QUIZ

Here are a few odd facts you really, really want to know about Oxford. But be warned … if you can't guess the correct answers you will probably grow up to be a teacher.

1 Oxford University grew quickly in the middle of the 1300s. For what horrible reason?
a) The plague known as the Black Death arrived in 1349. (That's true.) It killed so many there was a lot of spare land for new colleges.
b) The Hundred Years' War started in France. (That's true.) The new colleges were needed to teach the soldiers French.
c) Thousands of sheep died in a plague in 1349. (That's true.) Colleges were built in the empty fields.

2 Oxford has two roads called North and South Parade. Why?
a) Because they were full of pear trees and were famous for making a fizzy drink, 'pear-ade' – parade, geddit?
b) Troops marched up and down them, on parade, when Oxford was attacked.
c) Criminals were 'paraded' along there on their way to execution.

3 Nathaniel Conopios came all the way from Crete to be a student at Balliol College in Oxford.

He also brought a new drink with him … coffee. In May 1637 he became the first person known in history to serve coffee in England.

The idea caught on. All the students started drinking it. In 1651 the first coffee house in England opened in Oxford.

What happened to clever Conopios?
a) He died from drinking too much coffee.
b) He became the first person in Britain to make a million pounds.
c) He was thrown out of the university.

4 University men liked to sunbathe on the banks of the river at University Parks. They lay there with no clothes on. Ladies who went past in boats were told what?
a) Have a good look and a good laugh.
b) Show you are shocked – jump ashore and bash them with your brolly.
c) Look the other way. A teacher with no clothes on is not a pretty sight.

5 Why is the Bodleian Library in Oxford different to your library?
a) You are allowed to talk in there and even sing and dance.
b) You can't borrow the books.
c) The old books are so large, 37 people were crushed when a big book on a top shelf fell on them. (And 166 people have had their skulls cracked … but lived.)

6 Lewis Carroll created *Alice's Adventures in Wonderland* in Oxford. He also created the nyctograph. What did it do?
a) It let you write in the dark.
b) It cleaned your toilet without you having to touch it.
c) It pulled out teeth without hurting you (much).

7 In 1889, St Giles' Fair in Oxford had a ride where you grabbed a handle and slid down a wire to the ground. It was fun, but some people were banned. Who?

a) Policemen on duty

b) Children under five

c) Women

8 Edmond Halley (1656–1742) went to college in Oxford. He worked out that a bright comet visited the skies of Earth every 75 or 76 years. They called it Halley's Comet. Some said it was unlucky. Which dreadful defeat did England suffer when Halley's comet appeared?

a) The Viking massacres of AD 783.

b) The Battle of Hastings, 1066.

c) The World Cup, 1972.

9 Agnes Perone was just six months old when she died in 1392. Ahhhh! What horrible way did she die?

a) She was snatched by a sow.

b) She was crushed by a cow.

c) She was dropped in a row.

10 A cruel Oxford teacher died in 1301. He climbed into the branches of a tree. Why?

a) He was rescuing his cat.

b) He was catching a bird for school dinner.

c) He was gathering sticks to beat his pupils.

11 The Oxford English Dictionary was written by a team and took 70 years to finish. One of the first writers was what?
a) A mad murderer.
b) A bad butcher.
c) A savage surgeon.

And here's why…

1a) The plague came along … and if you were spotted you were dead[8].

About half of the students died. They caught the disease in the plague-filled houses of their teachers.

The monk Henry of Knighton said…

Many villages and towns have now become quite empty. No one is left in the houses, for the people are dead that once lived in them.

Farmers ran away from Oxford. If they died (or didn't come back) there was some nice cheap land. So it was decided new colleges should be built on this land.

8 Joke – spotted, plague spots, geddit? Oh, never mind.

Why new ones? Because students didn't want to go back to their teachers' mouldy houses. Would YOU?

2b) In the English Civil War (1642–51) Oxford was King Charles I's home. So of course the Roundheads attacked it. Charlie's troops paraded up and down the roads and they became known as North and South Parade.

The king's money store was said to be in a tavern called 'The Eagle and Child'. Its nickname was 'The Bird and Baby' or even 'The Bird and Brat'. It has a vicious pub sign showing a baby snatched in the claws of an ugly eagle. Cheerful.

The writer of *The Lord of the Rings* used to meet his mates in there. You can still visit it today, but be careful…

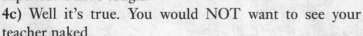

VISITING THIS PUB COULD BECOME A BAD HOBBIT

3c) Con of Crete was expelled. That's tough.

4c) Well it's true. You would NOT want to see your teacher naked.

5b) The Bodleian Library is not a 'lending' library. You go there to read a book but the book stays there. You even have to make a promise not to hurt the books.

I HEREBY PROMISE NOT TO TAKE ANY BOOK FROM THE LIBRARY, OR TO MARK IT IN ANY WAY. I WILL NOT BRING INTO THE LIBRARY ANY FIRE OR FLAME AND NOT TO SMOKE IN THE LIBRARY; AND I PROMISE TO OBEY ALL THE RULES OF THE LIBRARY

In the 1640s, King Charles I went to the library and said, 'I'm the king. I want to borrow a book.'

He was told, 'Sorry, the librarian is away.'

And every time he went to the library it was closed. Even a king can't break the big Bod rules.

Did you know...?
The Bodleian Library might ban 'fire and flame', but in 1641 a famous lantern was given to the library. It was the lantern the gunpowder plotter, Guy Fawkes, had been holding when he was arrested.

The lantern was passed over to the Ashmolean Museum in Oxford ... before the books caught fire!

6a) The nyctograph was a small machine that he used for writing in the dark, while lying awake. He said...

It lets you write a few lines, or even a few pages, without even putting the hands outside the bedclothes.

TICKETTY TICK TICK
Twas brillig and slithy toves...

Very handy if you're kidnapped and locked in the boot of a car. You can write a note, slip it out through a crack in the boot lid and maybe get rescued!

Really, everyone should carry a nyctograph with them at all times. I know I would ... if I knew where to get one.

At Oxford Lewis Carroll also invented:
- A travel chess set
- An early form of Scrabble
- A steering gear for a tricycle
- Rules for a win in betting
- Double-sided sticky tape
- And ... best of all for history pupils ... a way of remembering dates

Cool Carroll was also a poet, a maths teacher, a photographer, an artist and a preacher.

How did this man find time to write the *Alice* books?

Did you know...?

There is a story that says Queen Victoria read *Alice's Adventures in Wonderland*. She wrote to Lewis Carroll and said...

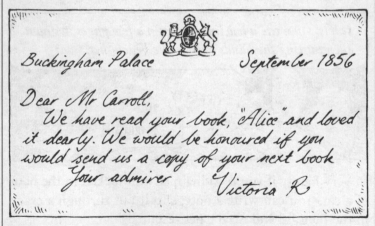

Buckingham Palace   September 1856

Dear Mr Carroll,
     We have read your book, "Alice" and loved it dearly. We would be honoured if you would send us a copy of your next book
     Your admirer   Victoria R

Carroll sent her his next book – it was a maths book. Victoria was NOT amused.

Of course Lewis Carroll always said that this story wasn't true. But it IS true that *Alice* was banned in China in 1934. The Chinese said it was 'wrong' to have talking animals in books.

7c) The local paper reported:

St Giles' Fair report

The flying trapeze is very popular this year. A thick wire was put up about 10 metres high and 40 metres long. To this was attached a handle with wheels, which ran swiftly down the wire. The public were invited to take hold of this handle and throw themselves from the platform. They felt as if they were flying though the air. At the end of the wire was a padded board to stop them being hurt and a net underneath in case of a fall.

Many people tried it. Not only men and boys, but on Monday many females, climbed the platform in spite of the things people said. After a time the owner of the trapeze was told that females must not be allowed to use it.

Why ban women? The crowds could see their knickers!

St Giles' Fair was a noisy funfair packed with the weird, wonderful and cruel…

Day's Menagerie
500 Animals, including
lions, tigers, leopards
bears, hyenas, pack of
wild wolves, ostriches
pelicans, vultures, owls
etc.

The Armless Wonder
a man born without hands
or arms who does all kinds
of work with his feet.

The Beauty of Adelaide
a woman of huge size

Dancing tent

Boxing ring

Carver's Champion Shooters
a man firing at apples, plums,
etc on a woman's head

Kasper and Tamora
the mysterious thought
readers

Sea on Land Cars
a merry-go-round
with sailing ships

Waxworks
with Lorenzo, an American lion
tamer, and the performing fleas

Swings

One of the favourite ways to have fun at the fair was to buy a feather brush. Young people ran around brushing other people's faces with them. A police report said…

In a few cases, where these were being roughly used, we took them away from the owners.

Spoilsports!

Did you know…?
In 1965 the most horrible thing you could see at St Giles' Fair WASN'T ladies knickers … it was 'The Man–Eating Rat'.

VERY FUNNY …… NOT

8b) England's King Harold lost the Battle of Hastings when William the Conqueror attacked. The famous Bayeux Tapestry shows people pointing at the bright light in the sky.

IT'S BAD LUCK

NOT FOR THE FRENCH

Halley went to an Oxford college but left before he took the exams. Seems like a good idea.

Horrible history happens … and people like to blame the comet! Here are a handful of cruel comet dates (apart from 1066).

• **1142** Matilda escaped Oxford in 1141 but this year her enemy grabs Faringdon Castle (32 km away). BAD luck Matilda – GOOD luck Stephen.

• **1222** Riots in the streets of London. The rebels want the French king to take over England from Henry III. BAD luck rebel leader who is hanged – GOOD luck for Henry III.

• **1531** Henry is setting up his Protestant Church. The arguments and violence will lead to hangings, burnings and torture in Oxford, as well as the monastery closing. BAD luck for all.

• **1682** The Duke of Monmouth leads a rebellion against James II. He loses and some of his rebels are locked in Oxford Castle. BAD luck for Monmouth, who loses his head – GOOD luck for Oxford jailers.

• **1759** Oxford's favourite composer, Handel, wrote a special piece for his 1733 visit to the city. But in 1759 he died. BAD luck for Handel – GOOD luck for people who like rock music.

9a) Agnes was in her cot when a wandering pig grabbed her by the head and killed her. Oxford was not the tidy city you see today. Pigs and poultry, sheep and cows were kept in gardens and often wandered in the streets. A vicious pig could be deadly.

10c) The teacher, John Newsham, wanted to flog his boys.

Boys in Magdalen School in the 1490s had to practise Latin by writing about their lives.

If one of Newsham's pupils had written a diary of the tragedy back in 1301, then it might have looked like this…

Dear diary, today we had a terrible tragedy. Our school teacher, Master Newsham, decided to thrash us all with the birch because Peter de Vere left a dead rat on his desk. (It was meant to be a gift. Peter's funny like that.) Master Newsham began thrashing the first boy on the register, Thomas Abbot, and the birch twigs begin to split. 'Copy out Psalm 34 onto your wax tablets while I collect more birch twigs', Master Newsham told us.

We went to the window and watched him march down to Magdalen Bridge over the River Cherwell. All the branches hanging over the river bank were dry and brittle. It has been a dry summer. The really springy, hurting branches hung over the river.

We watched, amazed, as he began to climb a willow tree and make his way out to the branches over the river. We counted as he cut ten, eleven, twelve whippy twigs. They do say thirteen is an unlucky number. As he cut number thirteen he lost his hold and tumbled into the water.

His heavy gown soaked up the water and dragged him down. We raced out of the classroom and down the garden to get a better look. Master Newsham was waving at us. Each time his head came above the surface he waved. We waved back. At last his head went under one last time.

We watched for another hour but saw no more of him. 'I think he's in trouble,' Peter de Vere said. 'Shall we go for help?' he asked. 'Give it another hour — just to be sure,' I told him.

11a) Dr William Chester Minor (1834–1920) worked as a doctor in the US Civil War (1861-65). The horrors he saw drove him mad. Dr Minor…

• Had to burn the letter 'D' into a soldier's cheek – the punishment for a 'deserter'.
• Saw men blown apart by cannon shells.
• Saw men burned alive when the grass on the battlefield caught alight.

When he arrived in England in 1871, he was going mad from the memories. He was sure a man called George Merritt had broken into his room. Dr Minor found Merritt and shot him dead.

The doctor was sent to Broadmoor prison for mad criminals. He was a good prisoner so he was allowed to build up his own library.

When the Oxford Dictionary was started he offered to help – but didn't tell anyone he was a prisoner at Broadmoor. James Murray was the leader of the dictionary team. One day he told an American friend that Dr Minor from Broadmoor prison was helping. He was in for a shock...

After 12 years Murray went to Broadmoor to meet Dr Minor. They became friends.

In 1910 Dr Minor was sent back to a prison in the USA and died 10 years later.

Did you know...?
When the Oxford Dictionary was started they thought it would be finished in 10 years. But after five years how far had they got? As far as the word 'ant'. THAT'S why they needed the help of men like Dr Minor.

SAVAGE STUDENTS

Students come from all over the world to Oxford colleges. Some of these students don't get on with the people of Oxford. And the people of Oxford don't always get on with the students. That spells trouble…

The riots of 1209

In 1209 a woman was killed in fights between students and townsfolk.

Afterwards two students were hanged by the townsfolk who blamed them for her death.

Some of the students ran away to Cambridge … but in 1214 they were invited back by the people of Oxford.

In the 1200s there were at least seven sets of riots. But the worst was yet to come…

St Scholastica Day riot – 10 February 1355

Two scholars, Walter Sprynghouse and Roger de Chesterfield, visited the Swindlestock Tavern on Carfax. They were angry … or maybe just drunk!

The students threw the wine in the landlord's face and beat him. Other students joined in and a riot spread through the city. Students set fire to houses and robbed shops.

The townspeople fought back with bows and the first deaths happened. Two thousand country friends of the townspeople marched to Oxford with black banners. They chanted…

Slay, Slay, Havoc, Havoc, Strike fast, Give good knocks!

The mob invaded the colleges. Students were beaten and 63 of them were killed.

The students wore their hair like monks. So the town mob grabbed the front of the hair and SCALPED them. Students were thrown bald and bleeding into prison. Hair today, gone tomorrow.

After two days the mayor of Oxford rode to Woodstock, where King Edward III was staying. But the king took the side of the students and let them off their crimes. King Ed punished the townspeople, even though 30 of them had died during the riot:

EVERY YEAR YOU MUST PAY A FINE – ONE PENNY FOR EVERY DEAD STUDENT – SIXTY THREE PENCE

Edward said the money would help poor students to go to college.

WE WIN: OXFORD ONE... STUDENTS ONE!

Scrapping students

The students never got on very well with the people of Oxford. But there were times when the students hated one another even more.

In 1388 two students, John Alkebarow and John Taylor, were dragged before the king, Richard II. They were accused of starting a small war in their college between two groups.

HE'S FROM THE NORTH SO I HATE HIM

HE'S FROM THE SOUTH SO I HATE HIM

CAN YOU AGREE ON ANYTHING?

YES... WE *BOTH* HATE THE WELSH

Alkebarow had been in trouble 10 years before. He'd been stirring up trouble with the Oxford monks and had been banned from carrying weapons.

COLLEGE CRIMINALS

Oxford is full of clever people. But in the middle of any group of clever people there are always one or two cunning criminals.

Sir Francis Verney (1584–1615)

King Phillip III of Spain threw Spanish Muslims (the Moors) out of Spain in 1610. Many went to North Africa and became pirates, attacking Spanish ships in revenge. English sailors often joined them, and became Muslims and pirates. In some ways it was a good life. Pirate leader John Ward was supposed to have written a poem to King James I:

Go tell the King of England,
Go tell him this from me,
If he reign king of all the land,
I will reign king at sea

Sounds good, BUT the pirates faced a horrible death if the Spanish captured them. They were tried by the savage Spanish priests – the 'Inquisition' – and could be sentenced to death by impaling.

A SHARP POLE WAS STUCK IN THE GROUND – A STAKE

STAKE FOR DINNER ENGLISH SEA DOG HEH! HEH!

This was the sort of horror waiting for an Oxford student, Sir Francis Verney.

Francis went to Trinity College and left when he was just 15 years old. He was fed up with his stepbrother, so in 1610 he sailed off to North Africa, became a Muslim and a pirate. He joined John Ward.

Then he was captured. Would he be impaled?

Francis promised to become a Christian again ... so he was let off with just two years as a galley slave – rowing great Spanish ships.

It was a hard life and by 1615 he was dead.

In 1622, Ward died of the plague.

Did you know…?
Sir Francis Verney left college at 15 to become a pirate. Sounds a bit young to leave college, doesn't it? In 1602 Sir Henry Mainwaring also passed his exams and left Brasenose College ... to become a pirate too. These young men started at Oxford when they were just 12 years old. Did they learn

piracy at college? Would you like to learn it at school? What sort of exams would you take?

ALL RIGHT, WAYNE, YOU GET TEN OUT OF TEN... NOW LET ME DOWN!!

John Clavell (1601–43)
This Oxford student had an odd sort of life, happy and horrible.

HAPPY	HORRIBLE
1601 Born in a posh Devon family...	Posh, but poor.
1619 Went to Brasenose College in Oxford...	Caught nicking the college silver plate and kicked out.
1621 The king pardons him (because of his posh Uncle William).	Struggles to make a living.
1625 Marries the lovely Joyce...	His family hate him because Joyce is from a poor and not-posh family.
1626 Becomes a highwayman to make some money...	He is caught and sentenced to hang.
1627 Charles I is being crowned so he has all highwaymen set free...	Joyce dies.
1635 He marries again, becomes a lawyer and a doctor and a writer...	In 1643 he dies of a lung disease, aged 41.

You don't HAVE to be a thief to become a writer, of course. But it DID help John Clavell. He wrote a long poem telling young lads NOT to rob, and telling travellers what to look out for on the road!

It was a l-o-n-g poem so here's the general idea...

You young men who want to rob
Get yourself a better job.
Don't become a highwayman,
Or, like me, you'll surely hang!
(Yes, well hang I thought I would
But King Charles to me was good.)

Gents and ladies in, your coaches
Don't bear silver, don't wear brooches.
Back at home your purses leave,
Men in masks are out to thieve.
(My mask did no good of course,
'Cos the lawmen knew my horse!)

If Clavell had been really clever he'd have put a mask on his horse, of course.

Did you know...?
Clavell's second wife, Isabel Markham, was said to be just nine years old at the time of the wedding.

Laurence Shirley (1720–60)

Laurence Shirley was sad, bad and mad. He went to Christ Church College in Oxford in 1737. When his Uncle Henry went mad in 1745, Shirley became Earl Ferrers. It seems madness ran in the family. In 1752 he married, but was so cruel his wife divorced him six years later.

He kicked a servant hard between the legs because the servant couldn't answer a question.

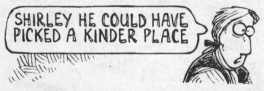

The doctor could see the problem.

Laurence was sure that someone was plotting to kill him – even though they weren't.

John Johnson had worked for the Shirley family for many years. He collected rents for them. Laurence started to think Johnson was one of his enemies. That led to the tragedy…

Johnson lay there all day, slowly bleeding to death.

The earl armed himself with a blunderbuss, dagger and pistols. The law officers were terrified. They sent in a gang of tough coal miners to arrest him.

They managed to grab him before he killed one of them. Because he was a lord he was sent to the Tower of London.

He said…

Shirley was hanged on 5 May 1760.

It's said he rode in his own, fine coach to the gallows and took his servants. He was dressed in a suit of white and silver … the clothes he was married in.

It is even said he was hanged by a silken cord instead of a rough rope.

Horrible Histories fact: Laurence Shirley, Earl Ferrers, is famous for being hanged with a silk rope because he was a lord. But that story is NOT TRUE. He was hanged with a plain hemp rope … the same as a peasant like you would have been.

He took four painful minutes to die … the hangman wasn't very good. As usual his corpse was cut up by the surgeons. Twenty years later his skeleton was sent home to be buried. The cruellest student of Oxford? Shirley he must be?

Did you know…?

The story of the silk rope may be untrue, but there is an even BETTER horrible story about Shirley's execution!

Victims usually gave the hangman a tip. Shirley handed over five gold pieces. But he gave the money to the assistant hangman by mistake.

The chief hangman, Tom Thurlis, wanted the money. The assistant said 'no'.

The two of them wrestled on the ground and fought over the money while Shirley waited to be hanged.

John Selby Watson (1804–84)

Another John, another Oxford man, another writer … and another villain.

John Selby Watson was born in 1804. In 1844, he became headmaster of the Stockwell grammar school in the London suburbs. A year later, he married Anne Armstrong.

He was sacked in 1870 for making his pupils work too hard! The parents just sent the kids to easier schools.

SACK TEACHERS WHO MAKE THEIR PUPILS WORK TOO HARD? WHAT A COOL IDEA!

A year after he was sacked from teaching, John killed his wife. He wrote a very long confession, then drank poison. The confession explained what he'd done…

To the officers of the law

In the living room you will find the body of my wife, Anne. She is dead.

I first met her in 1827, when I was just 23 years old and she was much older. She had money, of course, so in 1845 I visited her and proposed marriage.

For 25 years I put up with the old misery. I never even got my hands on her money. She kept her purse as tight as a corpse's fist.

You know I lost my teaching job last year. It was the fault of the pupils. They were not as brilliant as me no matter how I forced and beat and bullied them!

Without a job I had no money. After 25 years not even a pension. Still Anne wouldn't let me have more than a few pennies.

This Sunday afternoon, after church, we came back to this bleak boarding house. A failure, she called me, I have published books. A failure, she sneered. I was respected in Oxford. A failure.

I went and fetched my pistol. You will see I didn't shoot her. I clubbed her frail, white-headed skull. She died without a sound, without a word, without pain.

And now I will take this poison and save you all the trouble of hanging me. I escape the misery of life but I will not escape justice. I am my own judge and executioner.

Goodbye.
John Selby Watson

In fact the poison didn't work!

Watson recovered and went to trial. The judge sentenced him to hang. In the end he was sentenced to life in prison. He died there in prison at the age of 80. That taught him a lesson. Just think: a murderous schoolmaster. A teacher more terrible than even my history teacher!

Poisonous prince and murderous mate

Felix Yusupov (born 1887) was one of Oxford's oddest students. He ran away from Russia after he upset his dad... Dad found out that Felix liked to dress up in his mum's clothes.

The parties in his Oxford rooms were famous. They were shared with his pet – a bear cub that played under the dining table while he ate his dinner.

Felix may have been a prince but you would NOT want his Oxford life. He said...

I suffered terribly from the cold. There was no way of heating my bedroom, and its temperature was the same as out of doors. Water froze in my wash-basin, and when I rose in the morning the carpet was so damp that I felt as though I were walking through a marsh.

Still, he had a real live teddy bear to cuddle in his cold bed! Felix went back to his palace in Russia and took part in the murder of the mad monk Rasputin. Felix SAID...

FIRST I GAVE HIM ENOUGH POISON TO KILL SIX MEN, BUT HE LIVED...

THEN I SHOT HIM IN THE CHEST...

WHEN I WENT TO CHECK THE CORPSE HE JUMPED UP AND ATTACKED ME...

I RAN AND HE FOLLOWED...

MY FRIENDS BEAT HIM SENSELESS...

THEY TIED HIM TO A CHAIR AND THREW IT IN THE FREEZING RIVER

But every time Felix told the story he changed it. The TRUTH may be different.

The body of the monk had NO poison and he HADN'T drowned. He died from a bullet in the head. The bullet came from a British gun. The only man in Russia with such a gun was a British spy, Richard Dewdney. And Dewdney was an old friend of Prince Felix ... from Oxford.

Was one of history's most famous murders done by an Oxford student with the help of an Oxford man?

Dangerous place.

Ghastly goings-on

Every ancient city has its grim tales of terror. Are they true? Would you walk the ghostly alleys of Oxford after midnight? Here are some of the spooky sights you might see.

The Brasenose Devil

Place: Brasenose College wall on Brasenose Lane

Tall tale: In the 1700s, a priest called Churton was walking along here at midnight. He saw a cloaked figure pulling a student through a window – but the window was covered with a steel mesh. The shredded student was pulled THROUGH the mesh, screaming. The priest rushed into the college and found the president of the Brasenose Hellfire Club dead on the floor, covered in blood. He had burst a blood vessel. But no one could say how he got the bloody mesh pattern on his face.

CHURTON ALWAYS SAID IT WAS THE DEVIL IN A CLOAK DRAGGING THE PRESIDENT'S WICKED SOUL TO HELL

True or false? The priest's friends always said he was drunk at the time. But the members of the Hellfire Club DID try to call up the Devil. And their president, Edward Trafford, DID die that night. His death is still in college records.

The murder of Fair Rosamund

Place: The Trout pub, Wolvercote

Tall tale: Henry II (1154–89) spent most of his later life fighting against his wife, Queen Eleanor. Henry found a new girlfriend, Rosamund Clifford. Henry was so afraid Rosamund would leave him that it was said he kept her in a secret garden at Woodstock Manor. The garden was in the centre of a maze and guarded by one of his knights. The knight held the end of a silver thread which led to Rosamund. In 1173, the queen killed the knight and stole the thread. She found Rosamund and made her drink from a poisoned cup.

True or false? Another story says Eleanor stuck a thread to the heel of her husband's boot and was able to follow the thread to Rosamund's secret hiding place.

Sadly, it's about as likely as Snow White being poisoned by the wicked queen. For Rosamund died in 1176 – three years after Eleanor was supposed to have killed her.

Henry had Eleanor imprisoned in a tower from 1174 until 1189. She wasn't free at the time fair Rosamund died.

Headless Horseman

Place: Banbury Road, Oxford

Tall tale: George Napper was executed in 1610. His head was lopped off and his body cut into four pieces. His crime was being a Catholic priest. The four body-bits were stuck on the four city gates. Of course, old Napper's spirit went around collecting the bits together. But nobody knows what happened to his head – not even Napper. So now his ghost is doomed to ride up and down Banbury Road looking for it.

True or false? Think about it. How can you look for something when you haven't got a head with eyes to do the looking? The biggest danger in Banbury Road at midnight is a drunken driver, not a headless horseman. Read more about Napper's story on page 91.

Damp-faced dad

Place: Christ Church, Oxford

Tall tale: As you know, Lewis Carroll was a maths teacher in Oxford and he wrote *Alice's Adventures in Wonderland*. He wrote them for little Alice Liddell. Alice was born in 1852 and died in 1934, so you can't see her in Oxford today. But you can see the ghost of her father, who was head of Christ Church. He died in 1898, but his ghastly face can be seen on the south wall of the cathedral in damp weather.

True or false? A holy place would be a peaceful haunt for a ghost. You'll just have to go to Oxford on a damp day and look at the wall of the south aisle. If you see the face ask it, 'Are you a Liddell bit ghostly?'

The mystery monks

Place: The Chequers pub, High Street

Tall tale: It is said there is a secret tunnel that linked The Chequers pub to The Mitre pub in the High Street. This tunnel was used by the monks of Oxford in the Middle Ages. Maybe they were sneaking out for a pot of ale or maybe they were stealing. Anyway, someone blocked off the doors at each end of the tunnel. The monks starved to death.

True or false? Digging a secret tunnel is hard work. Who would bother? And why? The monks would have to be muddy mad.

AWFUL FOR ANIMALS

History can be horrible for humans ... but even worse for animals. Oxford has been terrible to turtles, horrible to horses and foul to flies. Swat up on these stories[9].

Batty Buckland 1
William Buckland (1784-1856) was a professor at Oxford who collected fossils and bones.

He liked to cover his desk with fossils of dinosaur poo.

He discovered the bones of a human in a Welsh cave and declared:

I HAVE NAMED THEM THE RED LADY OF PAVILAND: THEY ARE THE BONES OF A ROMAN LADY WHO WAS BURIED ALONG WITH THE BONES OF ANIMALS

They were the bones of a 25-year-old man and he had died thousands of years before the Romans came to Britain. But never mind, Will ... carry on.

THESE ANIMAL BONES ARE THE BONES OF ANIMALS DROWNED IN NOAH'S FLOOD

Fine if you believe the old legend about Noah and his ark. Will Buckland was a bit better with dinosaur bones. And he did some strange experiments. You can try this one...

9 Swat ... flies ... geddit? Oh, never mind.

Buckland's lectures on dinosaurs were very popular – he told lots of jokes and he used to show the students how dinosaurs walked ... by doing the walks himself!

William let guinea pigs and jackals roam about in his office. His horse was said to eat at the dining table with the family. When his students had turtle soup for supper, William Buckland's children rode around on the back of the turtle ... before it was sent to the kitchens.

Buckland WASN'T mad … until he fell off a coach and smacked his head. It made him mentally ill and he ended his life in a madhouse.

Batty Buckland 2

It was no wonder William's son, Frank Buckland (1826–80), grew up with an odd hobby … eating every animal, insect or bird he could get his teeth into. His dinner parties become famous for their toasted mice and chilled insects.

So which of the following tasty treats did the bloodthirsty Buckland eat? (Clue: FOUR are false.)

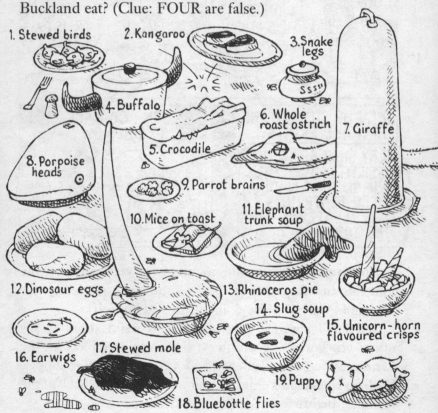

1. Stewed birds
2. Kangaroo
3. Snake legs
4. Buffalo
5. Crocodile
6. Whole roast ostrich
7. Giraffe
8. Porpoise heads
9. Parrot brains
10. Mice on toast
11. Elephant trunk soup
12. Dinosaur eggs
13. Rhinoceros pie
14. Slug soup
15. Unicorn-horn flavoured crisps
16. Earwigs
17. Stewed mole
18. Bluebottle flies
19. Puppy

Answers: Frank Buckland ate them all except 3 (snakes don't have legs), 9, 12 and 15. He DID try to eat 17 and 18 but said they were the only things too nasty to swallow. Earwigs were 'bitter' (he said).

And one day his friends saw a nasty stain on his doorstep. 'What is it?' someone asked. Buckland knelt down and tasted the brown stuff. Then he stood up and told them. 'Bat droppings!'

And when he was passing London Zoo he heard the leopard had died and been buried. He rushed in and asked if he could dig it up and cook it. The zoo said 'yes', so that's what he did.

Did you know...?
Frank Buckland also got his hands on the dried-out heart of King Louis XIV – stolen by grave robbers. Dad, William Buckland, had bought the heart and it was very precious.

One evening Buckland was having dinner with friends when he said...

He swallowed it.

And…

…one day in London when the grave of the poet Ben Jonson was disturbed by a nearby grave being dug, Buckland stole Jonson's heel bone.

Bad for bears

The Bear pub in Alfred Street was built in 1242 and they say it is the oldest pub in Oxford. It probably stood next to the Bear Garden and sold ale to thirsty crowds … or even 'bloodthirsty' crowds in Tudor times.

The Bear Garden wasn't a place where you took your teddy bear for a picnic. It was a place where you paid to see bears being 'baited'.

How do you 'bait' a bear?

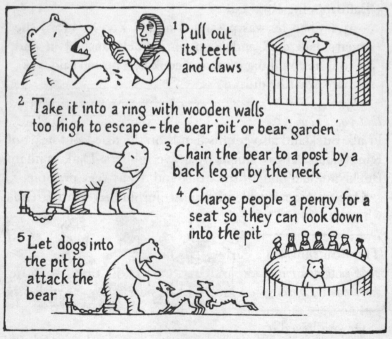

1 Pull out its teeth and claws

2 Take it into a ring with wooden walls too high to escape – the bear 'pit' or bear 'garden'

3 Chain the bear to a post by a back leg or by the neck

4 Charge people a penny for a seat so they can look down into the pit

5 Let dogs into the pit to attack the bear

A Dutch visitor, Desiderius Erasmus (1466–1536), said…

There are many herds of bears kept in England just to be baited. Sunday is the favourite day for these sports.

MOO

Parliament tried to ban bear-baiting on a Sunday … but Queen Elizabeth I loved it so much she made sure it carried on. She often watched a dozen bears being tormented in one afternoon 'show'. Paul Hentzner, a German visitor to Elizabeth's England said…

It sometimes happens they are killed on the spot; fresh ones are put in the place of those that are wounded or tired.

HE'S DEAD ON HIS FEET

He also describes the whipping of a blinded bear for 'fun'.

Did you know…?
The Bear pub had a curious custom.

If you went into the pub and cut off the tip of your tie, they would give you a free pint of beer[10]. On the wall you can now see old tie bits from famous people.

10 Sorry, I meant to say IF you were over 18. If you are under 18 you may get a free pint of lemonade … or water … or nothing.

Getting the bird

At Magdalen College there is an old record book that shows how its money was spent. One page written in 1491 says...

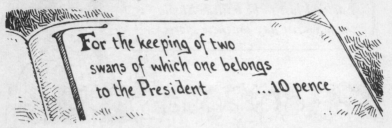

For the keeping of two swans of which one belongs to the President ...10 pence

Ten pence was a lot of money in those days. Did the president love swans that much? Yes.

Why? Because roast swan was very tasty on his dinner table. At least they had a good life, swanning around on the river, and their deaths were useful.

But a pair of peacocks was sentenced to death in 1856 because the head of the college hated their squawking! He said...

THEIR SINGING IS NOT IN TUNE WITH THE MUSICAL TASTE OF THE COLLEGE

SAY WHAT YOU LIKE. I'M NOT PROUD

At least a pair of emus were loved for themselves. They were sent to Magdalen College in 1884 as pets. One died on the journey. The other one was very popular. (It must have been a very emusing bird.) Too popular. It was found dead and everyone was upset. It was cut open to see how it died. It had died from being fed too much currant cake.

Many Oxford colleges in the Middle Ages decided it would be cheaper to keep their own animals to feed the students. Magdalen College had its own herd of deer that is still there. When the herd grows too large the deer are still shot and eaten.

Would YOU fancy a plate of Bambi and chips?

Rotten for rats

Professor Bobart was a teacher of botany. Around 1700, Bobart discovered a huge, dead rat in the Botanic Gardens where he lived.

With a knife and some twigs he chopped and changed it into a new shape. Then he told the world...

This is stupid, of course. But everyone believed him! Three professors wrote books about the Oxford 'dragon'.

Then Bobart owned up: 'Only joking!'

So did they rubbish the rat? No. It was such a clever fake it was kept in a case in the medical school.

Did you know…?

The first gardener at the Oxford Botanical Gardens was Professor Bobart's dad – an old German soldier, Jacob Bobart.

Jacob was a huge man who had a long, thick beard. One day a madman grabbed hold of Bobart's beard and cried out…

Did you also know…?

The Oxford Botanic Gardens were built on a grim, grave secret in 1633.

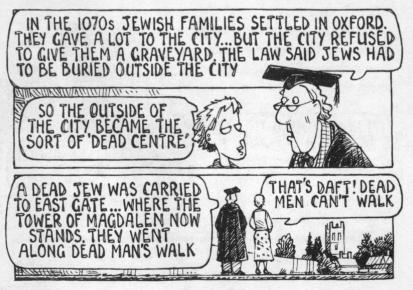

War for worms

The Oxford writer, Lewis Carroll, had some odd habits. He made pets of snails and toads.

He also tried to start a war among earthworms. He gave them small pieces of clay pipe for weapons.

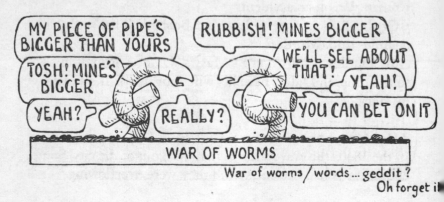

OXFORD DEAD

Oxford is a lively city ... if you're alive. But it has some dead awful stories.

1 An Oxford history mystery

Queen Elizabeth I (1533–1603) was famous for NEVER getting married. But people said she fell in love with the handsome Robert Dudley (1532–88).

The trouble was, handsome Rob was already married to Amy Robsart. Then Amy died. A story went around that she had been murdered.

• In December 1559 she had moved to Cumnor Place, 5 km from Oxford. Rob stayed in London.

• People said that Rob was trying to poison her. The poison didn't work.

• On 8 September 1560 she sent the servants off to Abingdon Fair. When the servants returned they found her dead at the bottom of the stairs.

• Did she throw herself down the stairs? Was she unhappy because Rob was flirting with the queen? Was it suicide?

• Or did she slip and fall? Some people say she was a sick woman. Was it an accident?

• Or did Rob arrange to have her pushed? That's what his enemies said. Murder?

Amy Dudley is buried at St Mary's, Oxford. Rob didn't go to the funeral. Did he have his wife murdered? It's a history mystery.

2 Bobbing bones

In the 1840s the graveyards were moved out of the city. Some churchyards had become so full they were overflowing.

REALLY overflowing. In a heavy storm the shallow graves were washed away. The bones at the top went floating down the streets of Oxford.

3 Sawing skulls

At Oxford Castle, 59 skeletons have been discovered – probably criminals who were hanged there.

DIGGERS ALSO FOUND THE SKELETON OF A CHILD ABOUT 12 YEARS OLD. HE SEEMS TO HAVE BEEN BURIED FACE DOWN. THE BOTTOM HALF OF HIS LEGS HAD BEEN BENT BACK AS IF HIS FEET HAD BEEN TIED TO THE TOP OF HIS LEGS TO STOP HIM STRUGGLING

HOW DO YOU FEEL ABOUT THAT, CHARLIE?

SICK

4 Rest in pieces

The trouble with being dead in Oxford is you don't always get to rest in peace.

Take the case of Katherine Martyr. If a newspaper had reported the case in 1554 it may have looked like this…

The Oxford Sun and Star

1554
1 coin

Free hedgehog pudding to all our readers - Collect the tokens

KATH CORPSE KIDNAPPED

Naughty nun, Katherine Martyr, has been snatched from her tomb in Christ Church, Oxford and she is one gone nun.

The German Kath was married to unpopular Protestant Peter Martyr. Poor Pete was boss at Christ Church but the Oxford people never liked wife Kath. They smashed the windows of his Fish Street house time and time again, till he was forced to move into Christ Church cloisters for safety.

Kath died in 1552 and Oxford people partied.

But Pete's bad luck was only just beginning. Our Catholic Queen Mary Tudor came to the throne and it was Pete who was 'throne' out of Oxford!

And it wasn't a case of forgive and forget for Kath. The Catholic Dean, Richard Marshall, is famous for his drunken habits and his filthy temper. He dug up the corpse and dumped it in his dunghill. It was carried on the shoulders of a labourer to his own yard, where it was buried among the filth. The labourer (who does not wish to be named) told our reporter, 'Bits kept dropping off as I carried her along – fingers, feet, that sort of thing. I had to keep stopping to pick them up. And she smelled a bit, of course – but not as much as she'll smell in the middle of Mr Marshall's muck pile!'

Richard Marshall said, 'It's a good day's work. The queen will be pleased to know Oxford is so loyal to her. Not even the queen's dead enemies are safe from Oxford's revenge. No one is crying over Kath's corpse now.'

The Oxford Sun and Star says, 'God save our glorious Queen'.

Of course Mary Tudor was dead by 1558 and the Protestants took over again.

Katherine Martyr's corpse was dug out of the dung. It must have been REALLY mouldy, falling to pieces, and smellier than a Tudor toilet by now.

She was taken back to the church and buried again.

Maybe this time she really could rest in peace. And they gave her someone to keep her company – St Frid…

5 Thick Thinne

Thomas Thinne was an Oxford student in 1666. He married Elizabeth Percy in 1681 when she was just 14 years old.

She ran away from her new husband and went to Holland – which is very flat. (It is easier to run when it's flat.)

Elizabeth's friend, Count Karl Johann Königsmark, sent three men to assassinate Tom Thinne. They shot him six times. As Elizabeth could have told you...

The killers were caught and hanged. Elizabeth wasn't.

6 Poorly pigs

In 1832 pigs were banned from Oxford.

The problem was that the disease cholera came to Oxford in 1832. There were pigsties all along the banks of a stream and their pig-poo was being washed into the Oxford drinking water. Forty people died and pigs were sent out of the city centre.

Still, cholera was back in 1849 and that time 64 died.

The pigs weren't the only ones blamed. At St Giles' Fair in 1832 a notice went up. It was meant to shock…

Apart from booze, toilets got the blame. Oxford toilets usually emptied into pits in the ground – 'cesspools'. These had to be emptied or they overflowed into the gardens and streets – heavy rain could wash out the waste and you'd be paddling in poo.

Doctors said…

THE CESSPOOLS ARE NOT EMPTIED OFTEN ENOUGH. THE SMELLS RISE UP INTO THE HOUSE AND CARRY THE DISEASE

But the doctors were WRONG! It wasn't the smell that carried the disease, it was the water.

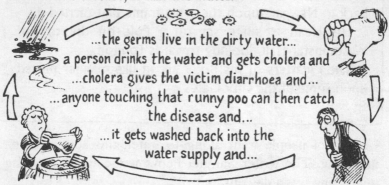

…the germs live in the dirty water… a person drinks the water and gets cholera and …cholera gives the victim diarrhoea and… …anyone touching that runny poo can then catch the disease and… …it gets washed back into the water supply and…

When the victim turned blue, they were as good as dead.

7 Napper – oil over Oxford

Queen Elizabeth didn't want her Catholic cousin, Mary Queen of Scots, to get the English throne. So Elizabeth made it a crime just to be a Catholic. Catholic rebels could be hung, drawn and quartered.

Liz died in 1603, but the law was still in force.

It was a cruel and messy business. A report from 1660 described an execution…

On Saturday 13 October 1660, between nine and ten of the clock in the Morning, Major General Harrison was dragged on a wooden frame from Newgate Prison to the place called Charing Cross.

A Gibbet was erected, and he was hanged with his face looking towards the Banqueting-house at Whitehall. Being half dead, he was cut down by the common Executioner.

His Privy Members[11] were cut off before his eyes. His Bowels were burned, his Head cut from his Body.

His Body was divided into Quarters, which were taken back to Newgate upon the same frame that carried it.

His Head is since set on a Pole on the top of Westminster-Hall, looking towards London.

The Quarters of his Body are in like manner placed upon some of the City Gates.

Crowds of people went along to watch this sort of man-mangling. The writer Samuel Pepys wrote about it as if a quartering was a day out.

11 Your 'privy members' are your naughty bits. Ouch.

I went out to Charing Cross, to see Major General Harrison hanged, drawn, and quartered; which was done there, he looking as cheerful as any man could do.

MUSTN'T GRUMBLE

Of course that was loathsome London. It wouldn't happen in Oxford, would it?

It did. In 1610, Oxford had its own hanging, drawing and quartering. The victim was George Napper.

His crime was being a Catholic priest. He was caught with some holy oil and ended up oil over Oxford.

The court was going to set him free but he made two mistakes:

• He converted a Protestant prisoner to Catholicism while he was in Oxford Castle jail. (Not very bright.)
• He refused to swear to be true to the Protestant Church. (Certain death.)

He suffered the execution between 1 and 2 p.m. One writer said Napper's noddle was stuck up on Tom Gateway. But another writer said it was placed on top of Christ Church steeple.

IS THAT ONE OF THE DREAMING SPIRES?

LOOKS MORE LIKE A DRIPPING SPIRE TO ME

YEUCH!

The four quarters of his body were put on poles on the four

city gates. But at least some were removed in secret by Napper's friends. They were buried in the chapel (now a barn) of Sandford Manor. Still the mystery of what happened to the head grew ... and became an Oxford ghost story (see page 72)!

8 Poison love

Mary Blandy (1719–52) of Oxfordshire wasn't ugly ... but she was what you'd call 'plain'.

Plain as a pork pie.

Still her dear dad, Francis, said he had £10,000[12].

Word of Mr Blandy's wealth went round. Lots of men told Mary that they loved her.

You know the sort of lover? 'Mary, oh, I love you ... madly ... can I borrow a few thousand pounds off your father Francis before I marry you?'

Dad always said, 'No, my Mary will get my money when I die.'

The lovers always went off in a huff with a 'Huh!'

Then Mary met Captain William Henry Cranstoun (1714–52). William wasn't ugly. He was horribly ugly. He was weedy and small and his face was scarred by smallpox.

William said, 'Mary, I love you ... can I borrow a few thousand pounds off your father before I marry you?'

And Mary told him, 'I love you too, my dearest darling – but Dad always says no. He says I will get his mountain of money when he dies.'

12 In fact the old man had THREE thousand pounds not ten thousand. But he liked to boast. The boast would cost his life.

William did something none of her other lovers did ... he said, 'I love you anyway!'

Mary was thrilled. 'I'll ask Dad if I can marry you,' she promised.

But Dad said, 'Mary, he is already married with a wife and child in Scotland! I forbid you.'

Mary was miserable. 'What can I do?' she asked the crumple-faced captain.

'Feed him some love powder!'

'Love powder, my love?'

'Yes. Put this powder in his tea and in his porridge and he'll love everyone – he'll love you and me so much he'll let us marry!' the crafty captain cooed.

So Mary sprinkled the powder in her dad's drinks and watched and waited.

'Ahhhh!' dad sighed.

'Are you in love?' his dough-faced daughter asked.

'No ... I'm in pain!' her dying daddy declared.

A week later dear dad was dead. The servants were suspicious. They found a packet with her powder.

'What's this?' the doctors asked.

'Love powder,' Mary told them.

'Arsenic poison,' the doctors said. 'This is murder, Mary, murder.'

'It is,' the servants said. 'We all heard mistress Mary curse her father. She said he was a rogue, a villain, a toothless old dog and wished him dead and at Hell.'

Mary was arrested and sent to Oxford Jail. She was made to wear leg irons whilst awaiting trial for fear she would try and escape.

At her trial, she shed no tears. And when the judge said, 'You will hang!' she went and ate a hearty meal. (Lamb chops and apple pie.)

She was executed in the Castle Yard in Oxford. At the gallows Mary showed a little fear. 'I am afraid that I shall fall!' she said (a funny sort of thing to say. She'd fall all right – the rope would stop her falling very far!)

And then she told the hangman, 'Please don't hang me high.' (She didn't want the waiting crowds to see her underwear.)

The ladder turned and Mary dropped. In minutes she was just as dead as her old dad.

But what, you ask, of wicked Will, her scar-faced love? He'd run away to France and left his love to hang alone.

He died just eight months later.

Serves him right, you have to say.

Epilogue

Oxford has always had a horrible history.

When peaceful Vikings tried to settle in the city they were massacred horribly. Is seems the people of Oxford didn't welcome strangers. So when students started to arrive there was bound to be trouble.

The students came and battled with the people. Students were scalped, townsfolk were battered, beaten and robbed.

One writer in the Middle Ages said...

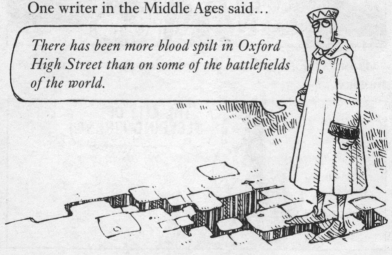

> *There has been more blood spilt in Oxford High Street than on some of the battlefields of the world.*

When the students weren't fighting the townsfolk they were fighting one another – the students from the north fought the students from the south ... just like football hooligans today.

The Civil War came to Oxford and the horrors of hanging, drawing and quartering. Body bits dripped down from the savage spires. More blood on t

And some of the students turned out and pirates, madmen and murderers.

Maybe most horrible was the tale of when the Tudors brought burning bishops to Oxford. The church and college spires would have been choked with human smoke.

Go to Oxford and see the dreaming spires ... but never forget...